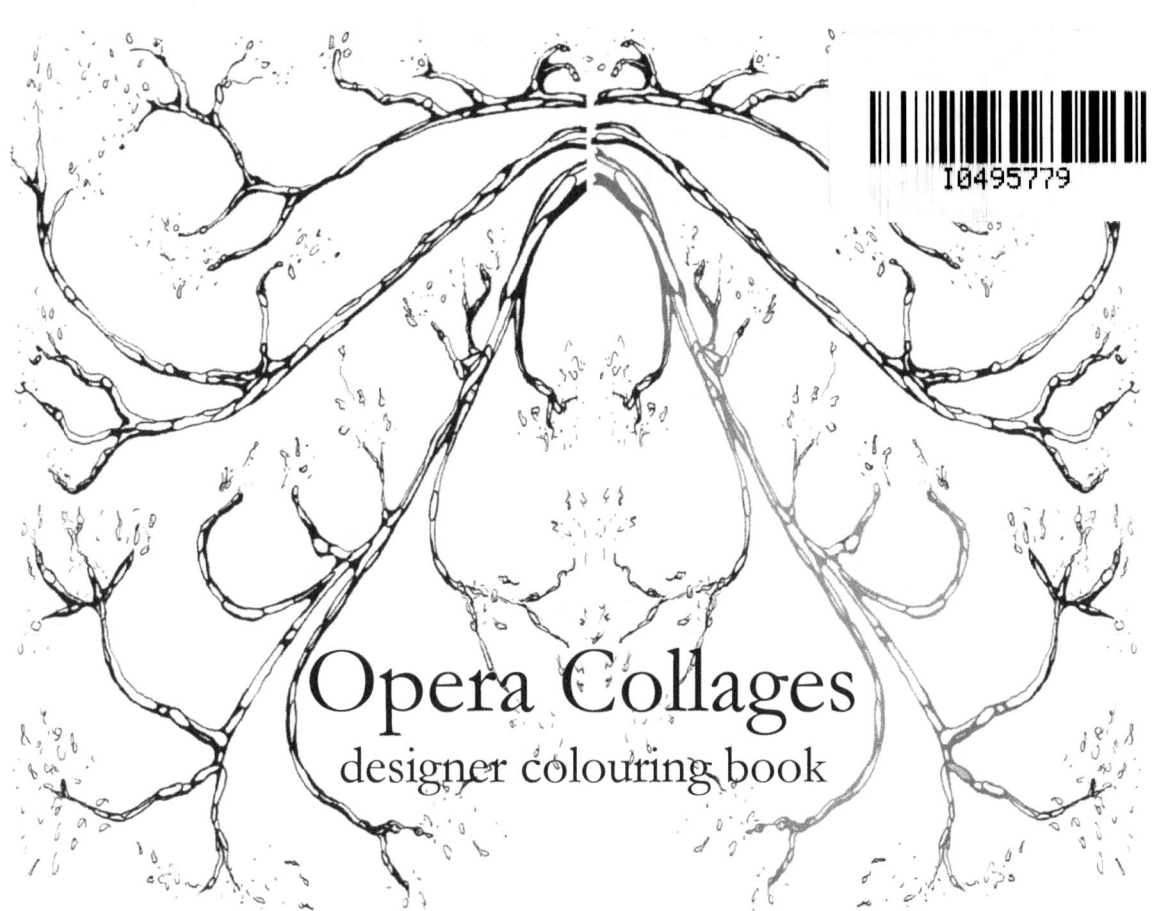

Opera Collages
designer colouring book

by

Hilary D. Slater

Copyright © 2013 Hilary Slater

All rights reserved.

ISBN:1493784498
ISBN-13: 978-1493784493

DEDICATION

I dedicate these drawings to children of all ages,
particularly those who have re-discovered their childhood later in life.

ACKNOWLEDGMENTS

I would like to thank all my Facebook friends for giving feedback on these drawings, prior to publication. I would also like to thank all the great teachers out there, -particularly Mr. Green, Mr. Anderson, Mrs. Huby, Ms. Tweedale, Mr. Marsh, Mr. Key, Mr. Smith, John Fillion, William Hodge, and Ruth Hay -to name the great ones who I have had the benefit of being taught by.
Great teachers are a rare breed, but so necessary if we are to develop students creative abilities.

I would also like to thank the Canadian Opera Company for presenting excellent ballet and opera performances. I produced the initial collage line drawings -in the dark- while watching the opera Carmen. I later developed these designs and created this colouring book.

Feel free to photocopy these drawings, but please include my web address/signature for copyright reasons.

1: THE HANDSOME MAN

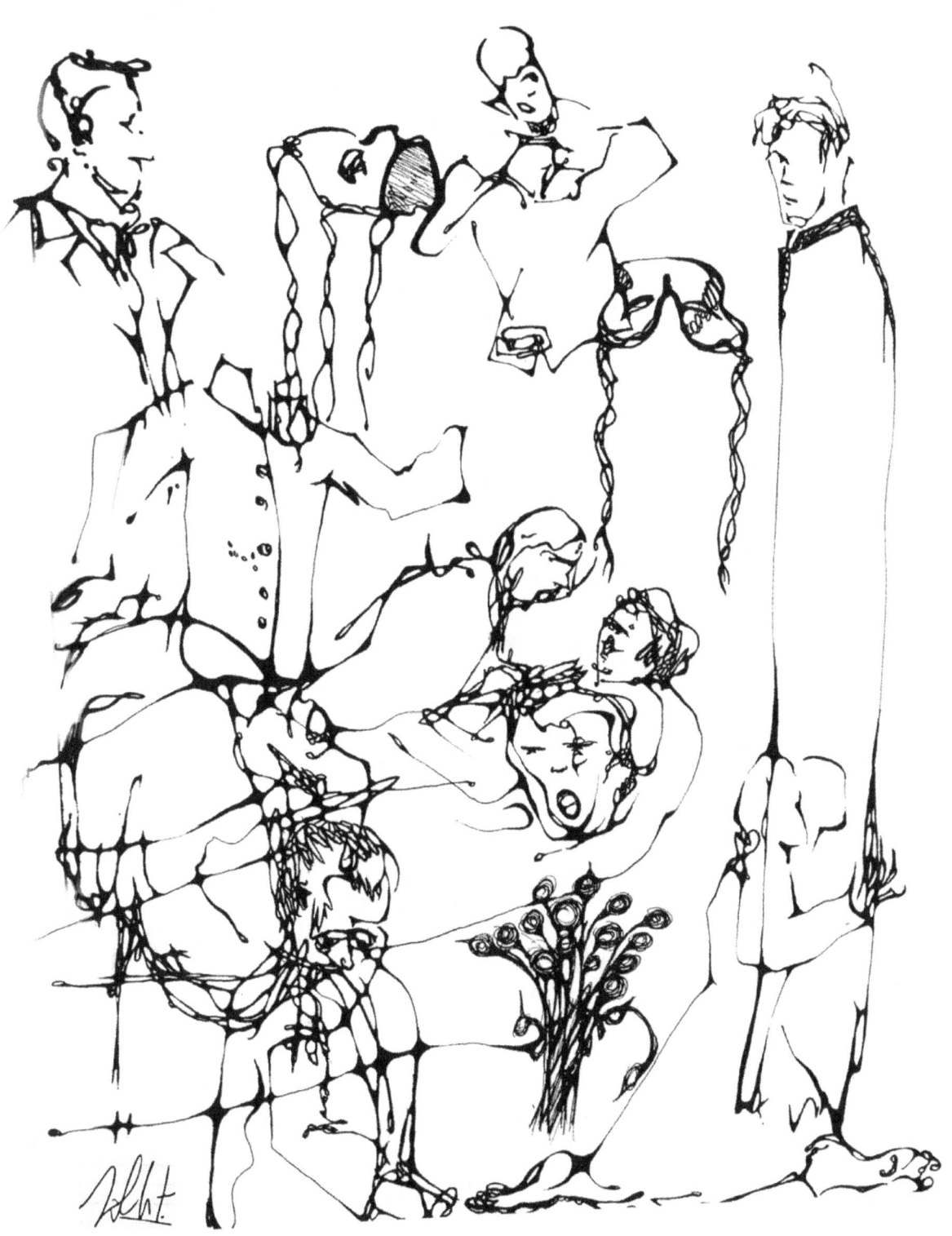

2: THE TOP HAT

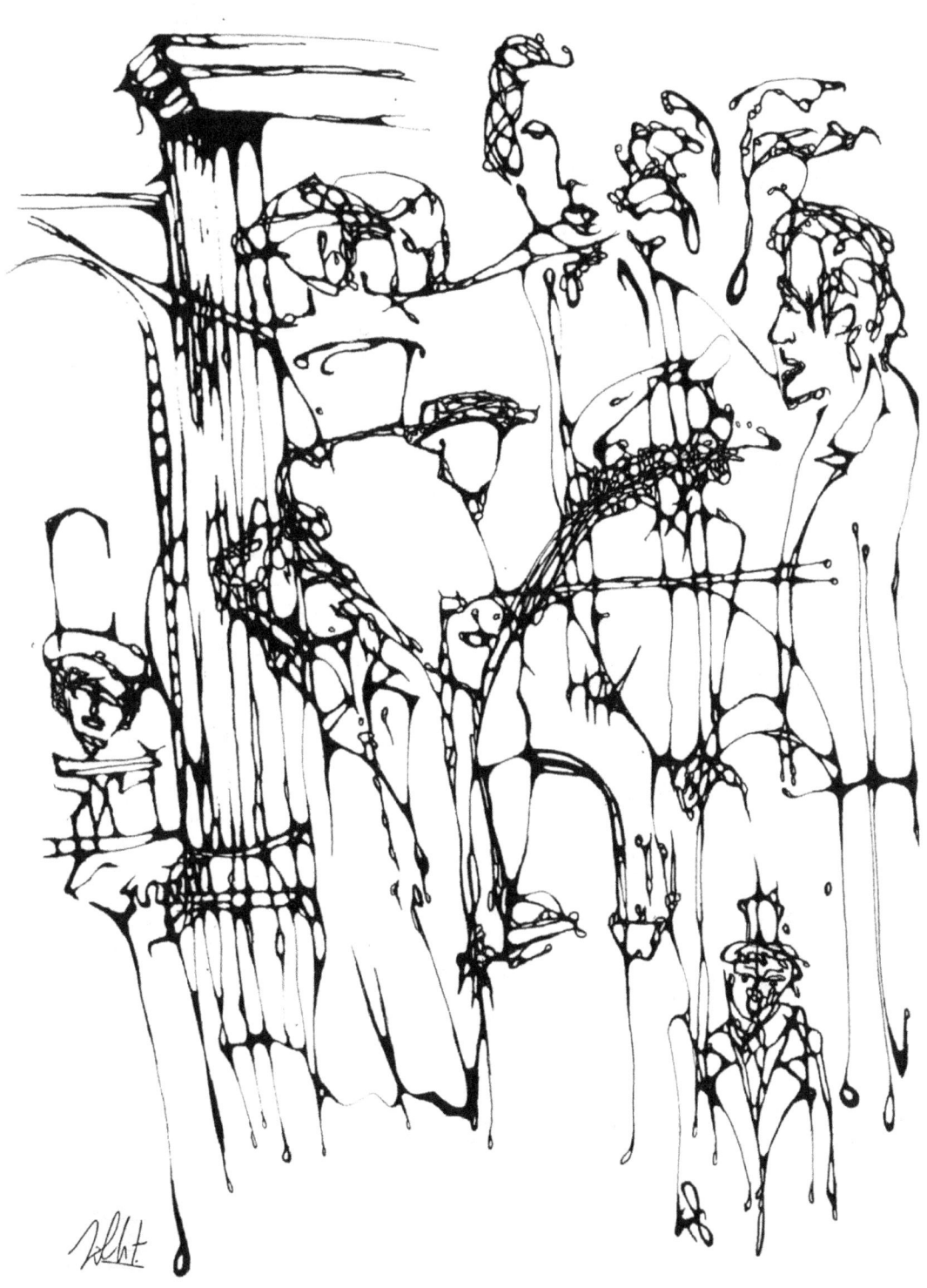

www.hilaryslater.weebly.com

3: THE BODICE

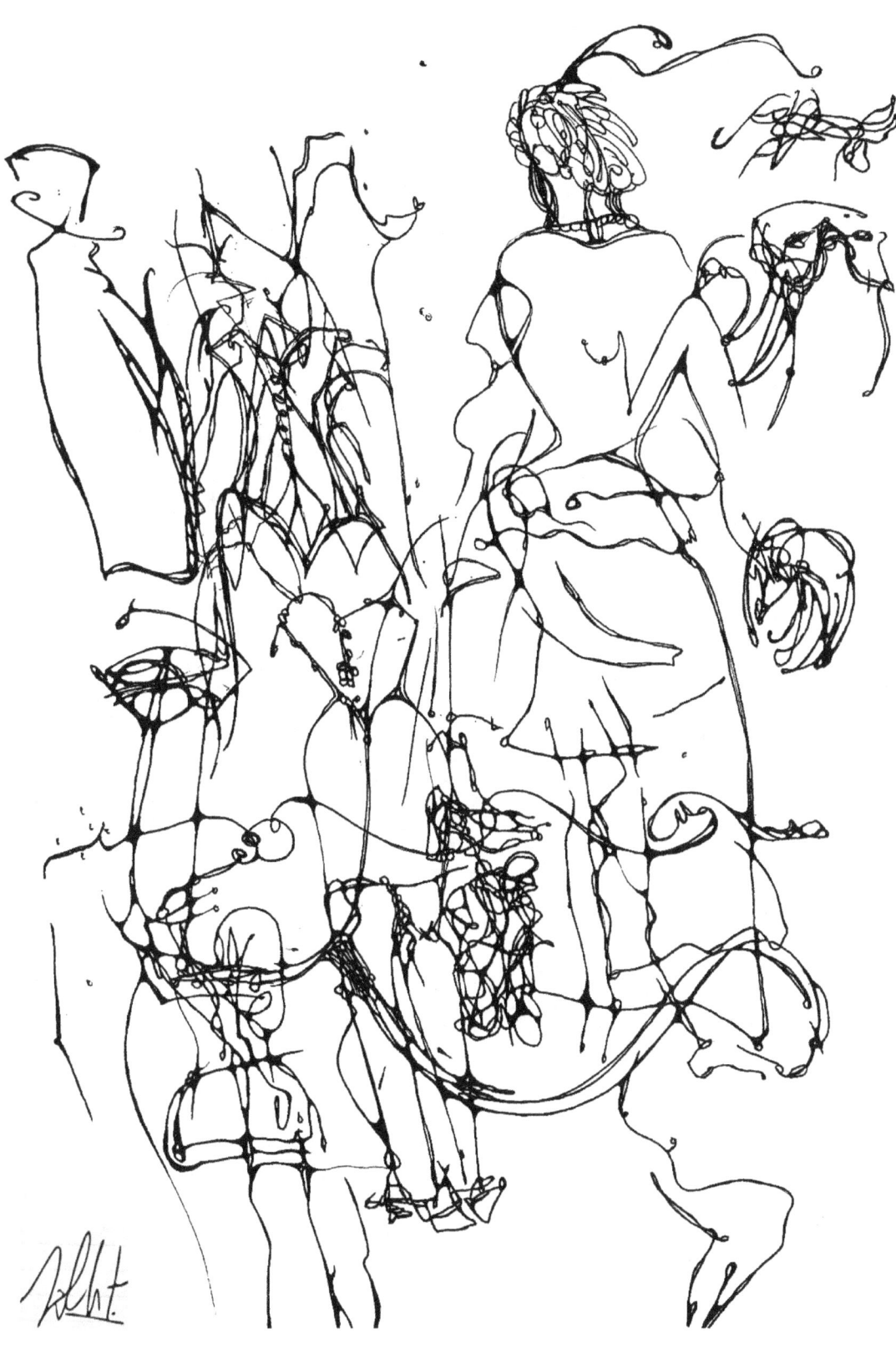

www.hilaryslater.weebly.com

4: THE FLOWER VASE

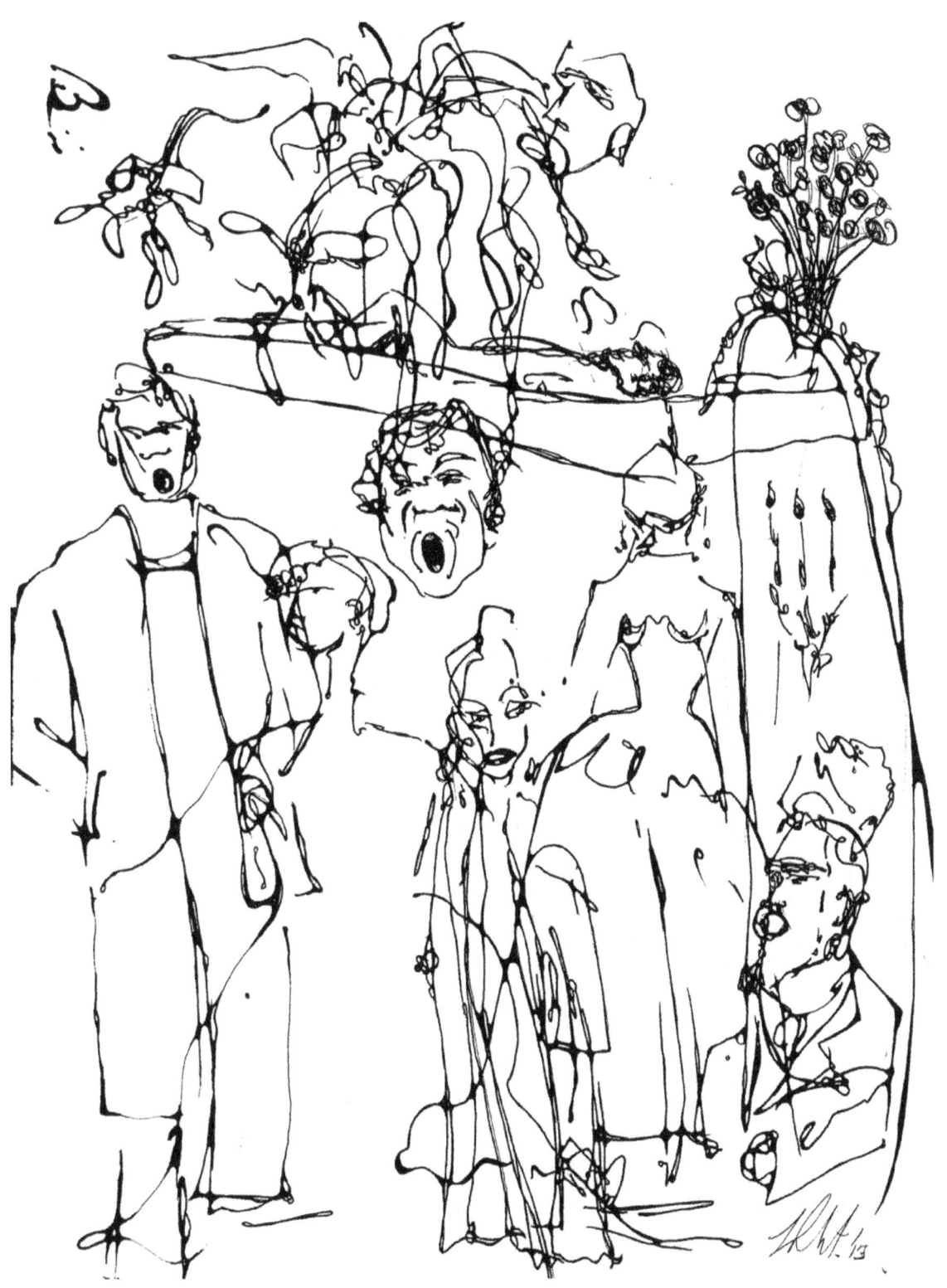

www.hilaryslater.weebly.com

5: LES TROIS DEMOISELLES

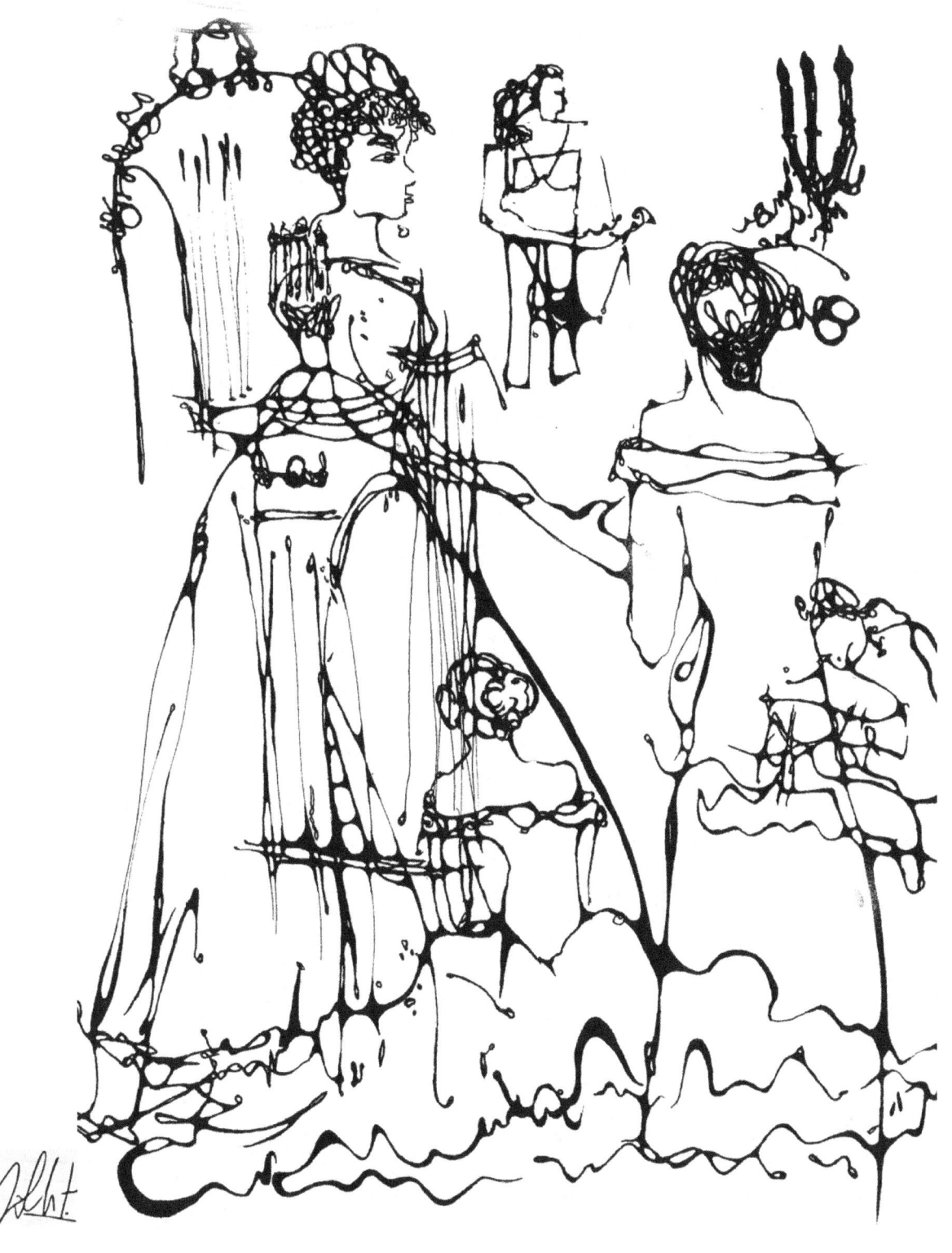

www.hilaryslater.weebly.com

6: THE TAMBOURINE

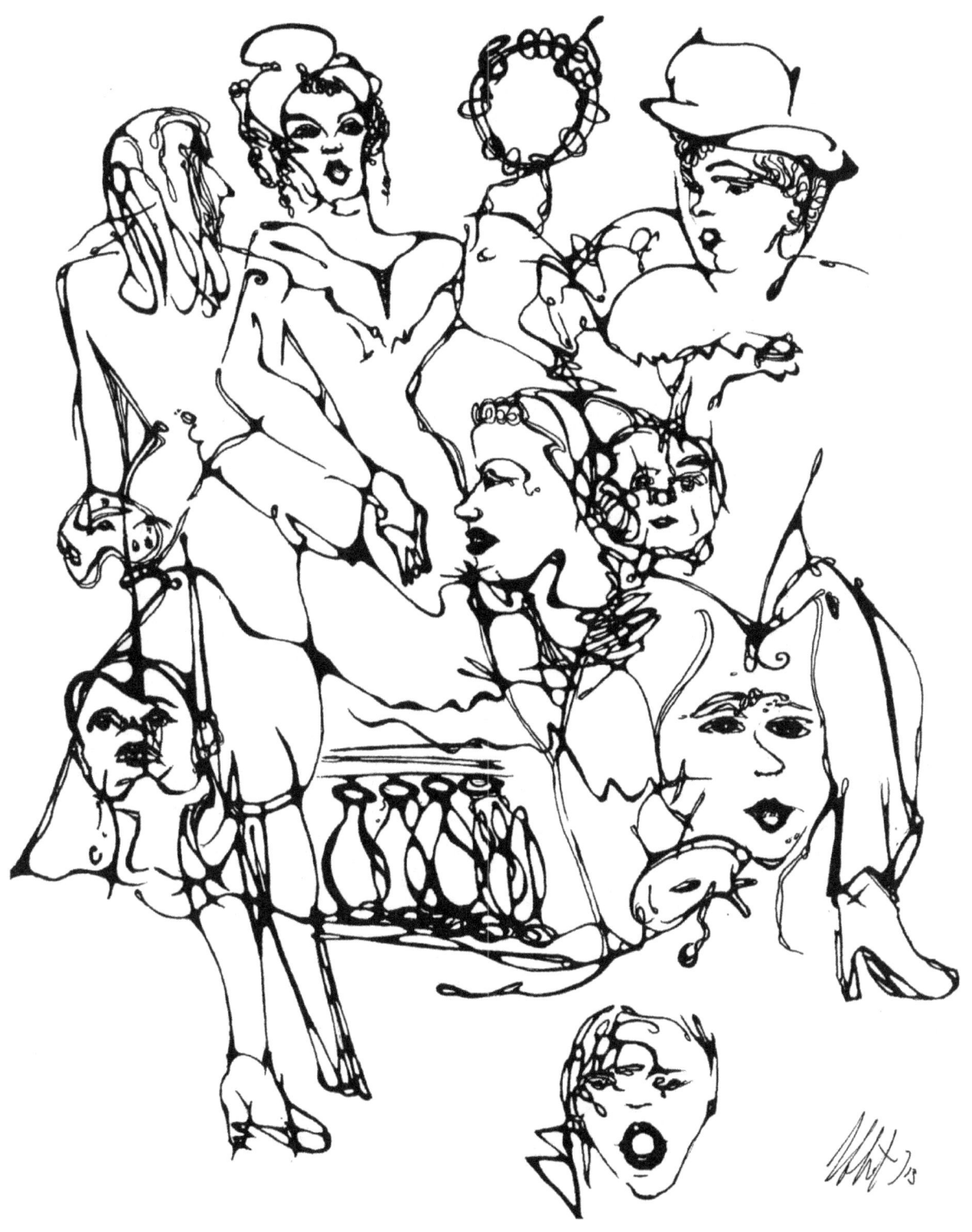

7: PEDESTAL PODIUM

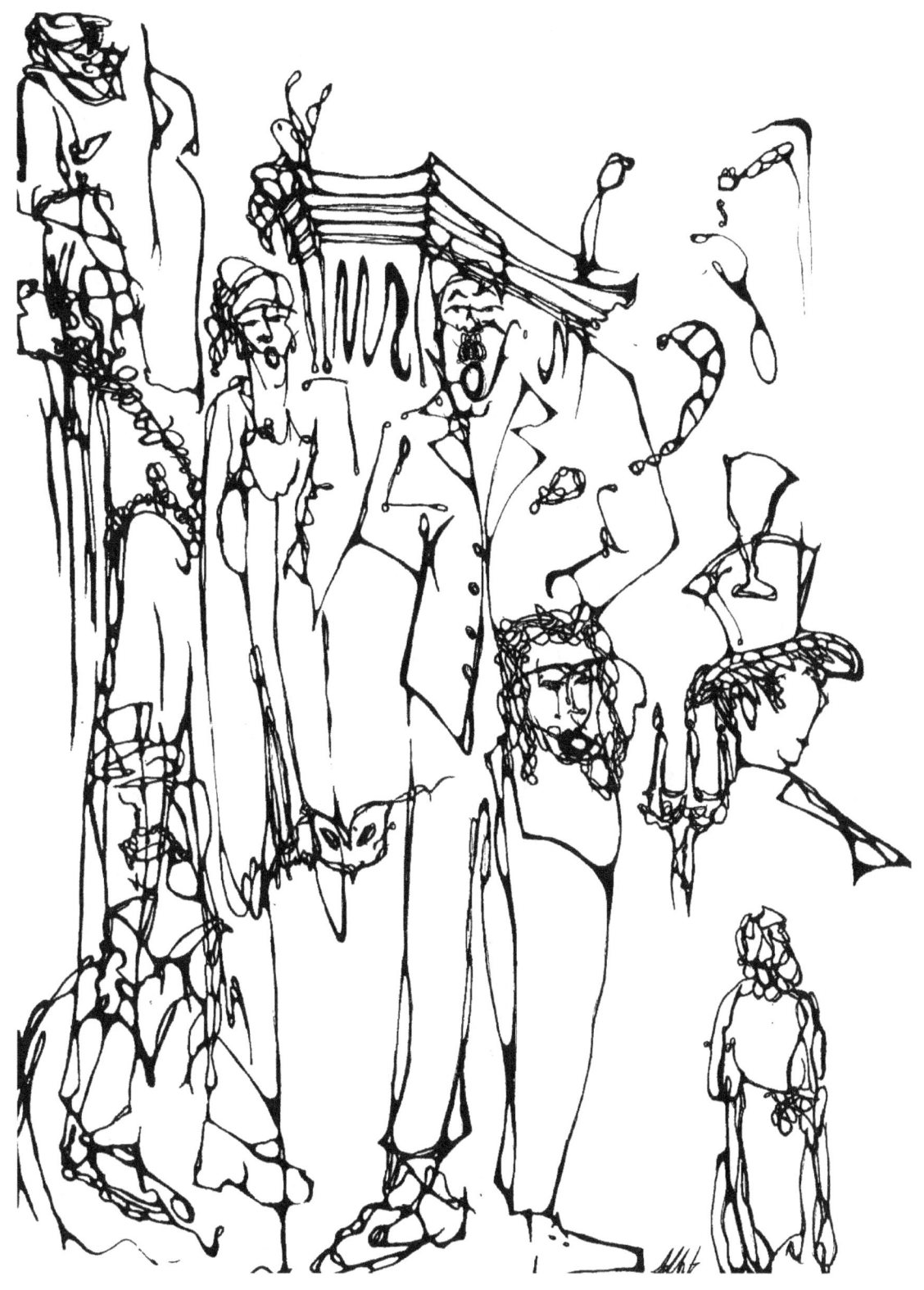

8: MUSICAL INSTRUMENTS

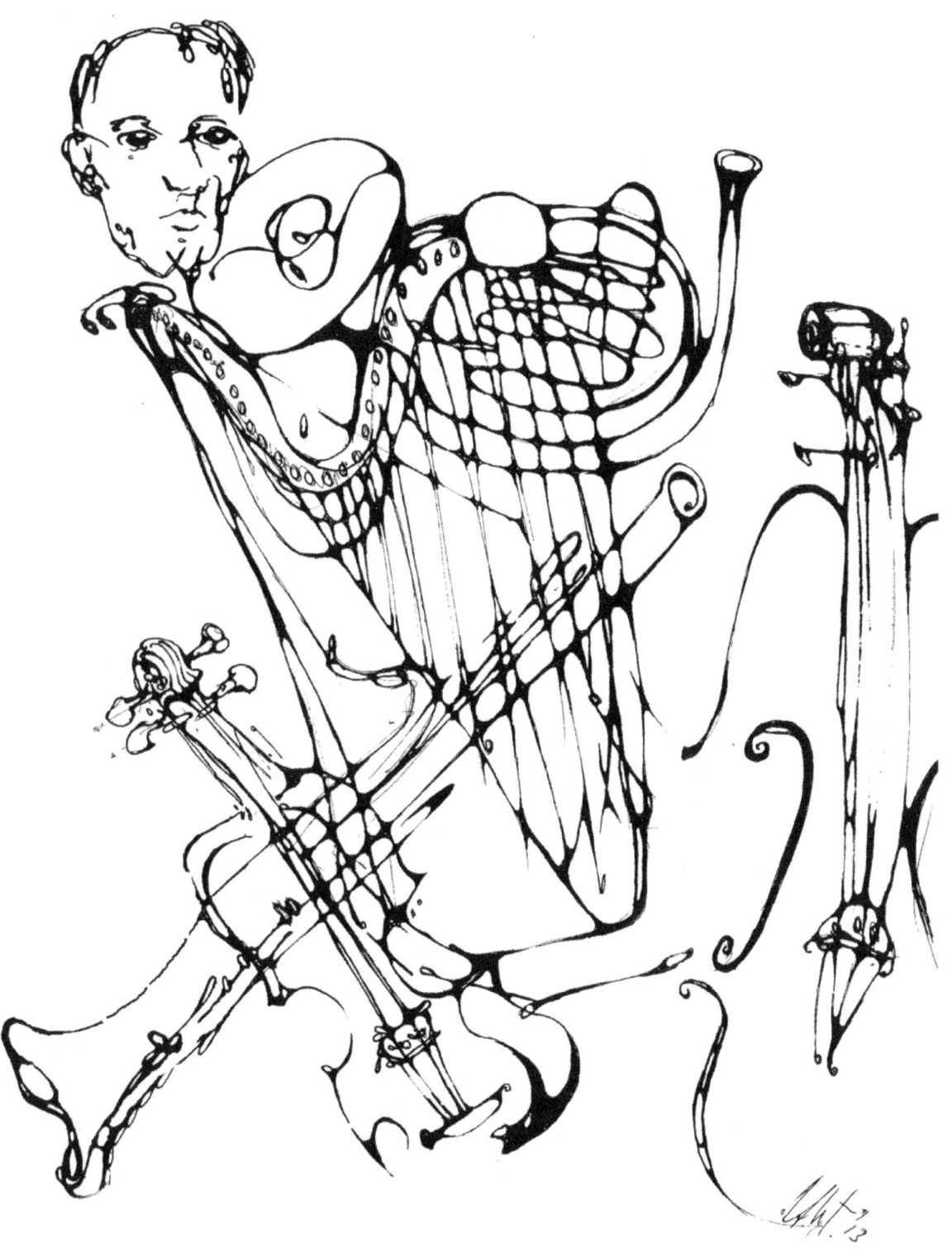

www.hilaryslater.weebly.com

9: THE PARTY

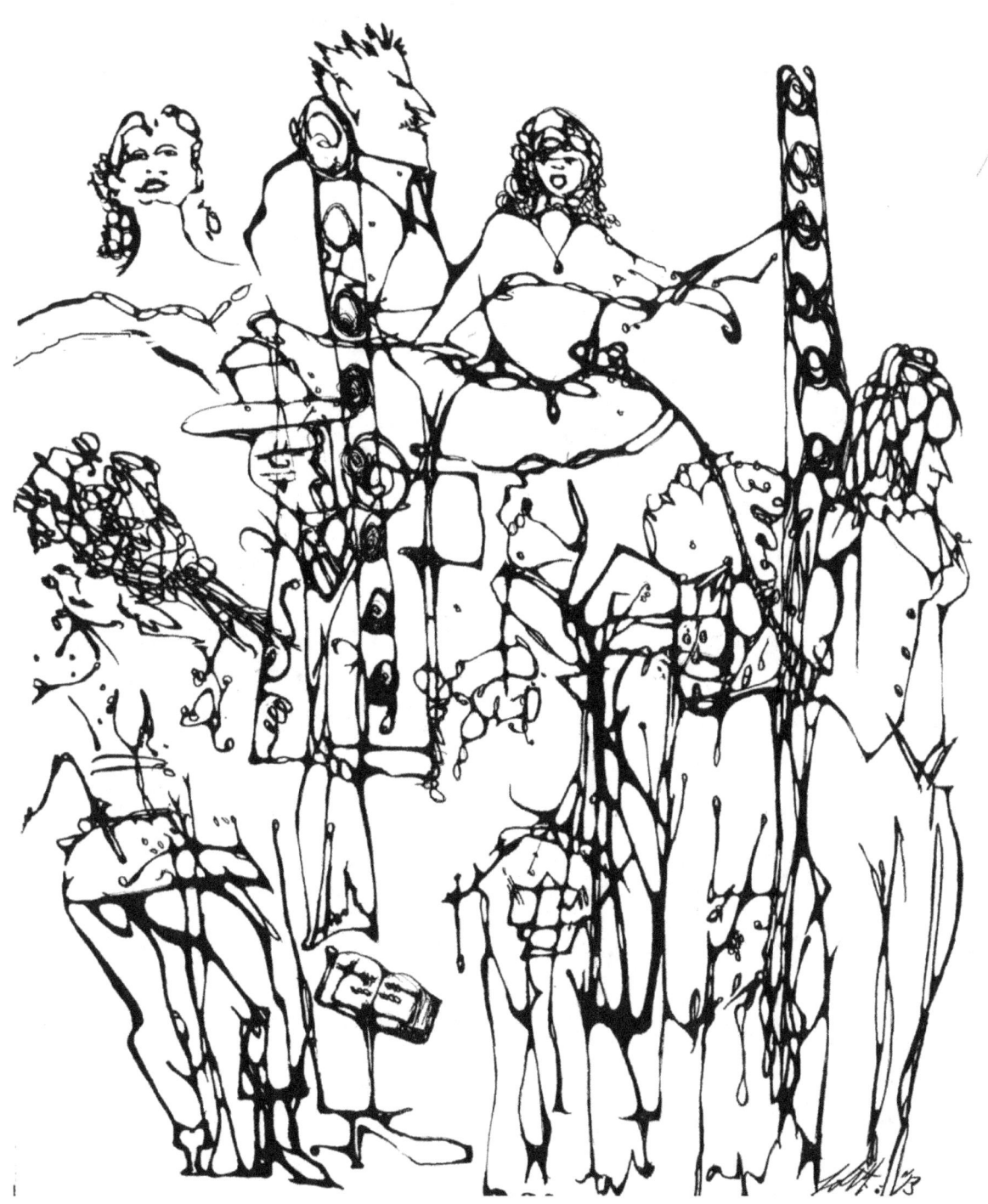

10: THE STAGE

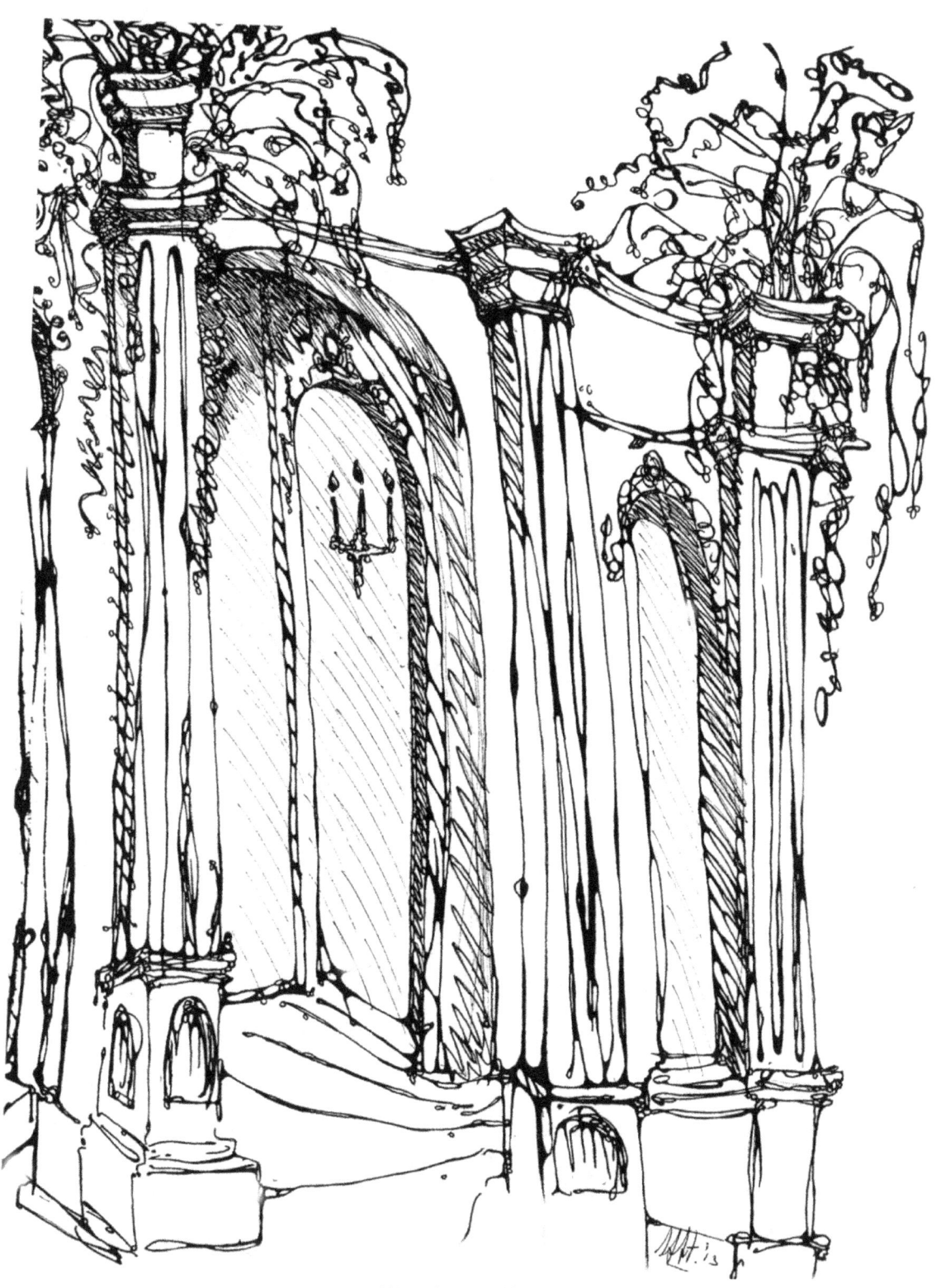

www.hilaryslater.weebly.com

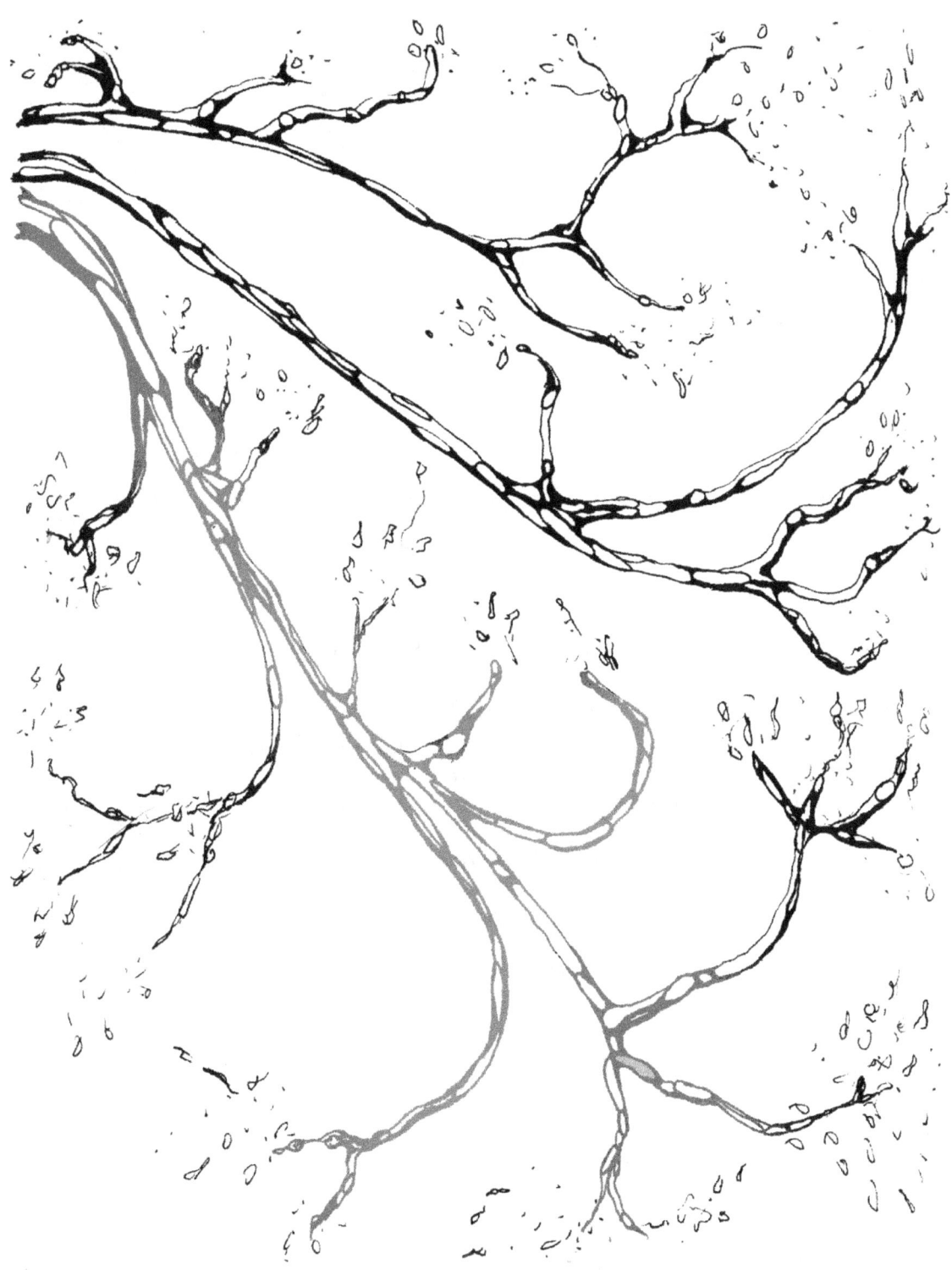

www.hilaryslater.weebly.com

HILARY D. SLATER

Hilary Slater is an artist, writer, landscape designer, potter, painter, pianist, cellist in training, and mother. The Designer Colouring Book Series is her newest project. Others in the series will be completed soon. Hilary has also written 24 novels to date, and is in the process of publishing them. The first novel, 'THE BIRD PEOPLE: Children of the Dragon' is now available on amazon.com. Hilary Slater has a website: www.hilaryslater.weebly.com She can also be Googled.

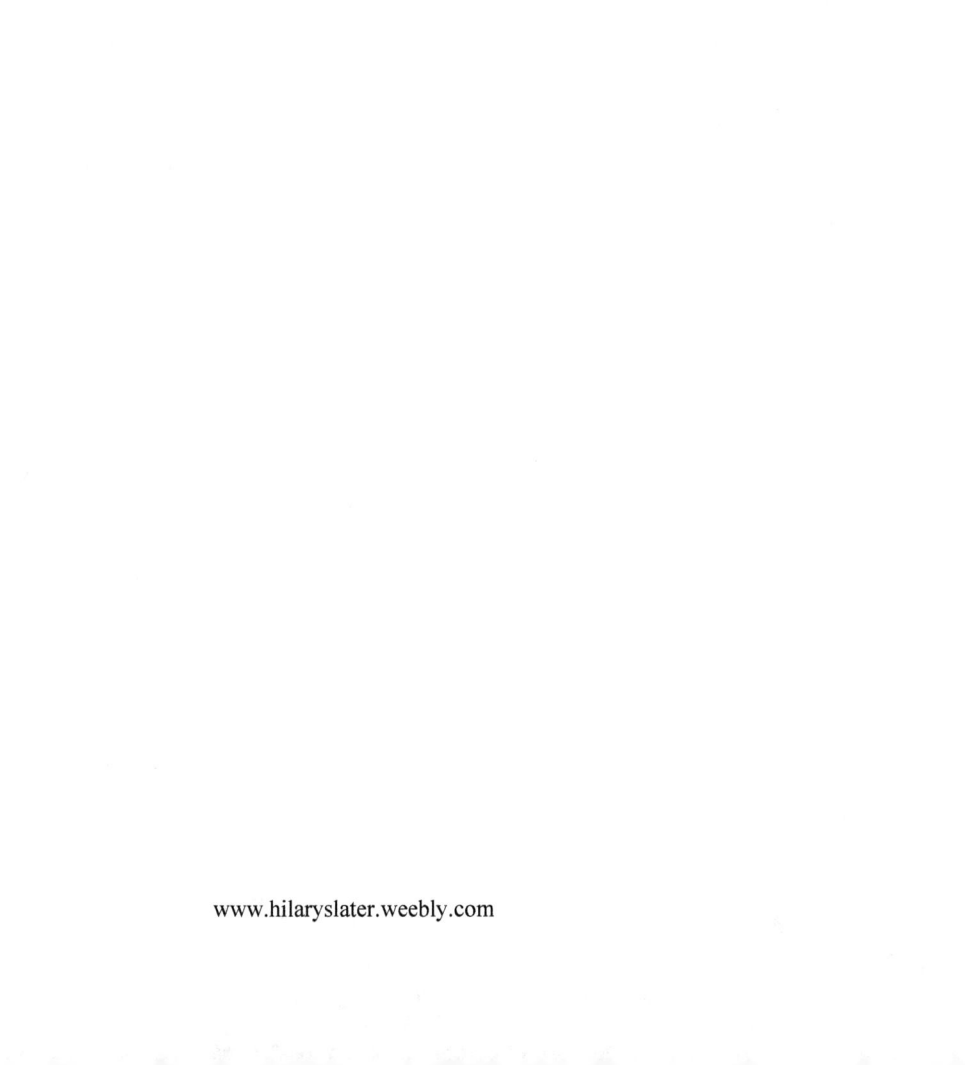

www.hilaryslater.weebly.com

www.hilaryslater.weebly.com

www.ingramcontent.com/pod-product-compliance
Lightning Source LLC
Chambersburg PA
CBHW081813170526
45167CB00008B/3426